PHILISTINE AND GENIUS

BORIS SIDIS

ALICIA EDITIONS

CONTENTS

PREFACE

WHEN in 1909 "Philistine and Genius" was delivered by me in the form of a Commencement address before the Harvard Summer School, my prediction of the coming European war storm was regarded by everybody as dream and fancy. My best friends and sympathisers thought my foreboding unjustified and ill-founded. I was an alarmist, a Cassandra, when I spoke of the coming catastrophe which was to shake Europe to its very foundation. When "Philistine and Genius" was published in 1911 the American and European press, dealing with the views advanced in this little volume, completely ignored the following warning given by me:

"About the middle of the nineteenth century Buckle made the prediction that no war was any more to occur among civilized nations. Henceforth peace was to reign supreme. 'The wolf shall dwell with the lamb, and the leopard shall lie down with the kid; their young ones shall lie down together, and the lion shall eat straw like the ox... Nations shall beat their swords into ploughshares, and their spears into pruning hooks. Nations shall not lift up swords against nations, nor shall they learn war any more.' This prophecy was rather hasty. We have had since the Civil war, the Franco-Prussian war, the Spanish-American war, the Boer war, the Russo-Japanese war, not counting the ceaseless wars of extermination carried on by civilized nations among the various semi-civilized and primitive tribes. Civilized nations do not as yet beat their swords into ploughshares, but keep on increasing the strength of their 'armed peace,' and are ready to fight bloody battles in the quest of new lands and the conquest of new markets.

"In spite of the Hague conference, convoked by the peace-loving Czar, no other age has had such large standing armies provided with such costly and efficient weapons of execution ready for instant use. The red spectre still stalks abroad claiming its victims. We still believe in the baptism of fire and redemption by blood. The dogma of blood redemption is still at the basis of our faith, and, consciously or unconsciously, we brand that sacred creed on the minds of the young generation."

The present European upheaval has finally disclosed to the impartial observer the fearful state of Europe as the final outcome of its "armed peace." Instead of realizing the dangers of armed peace or of "preparedness," we are ready to become a military democracy in which every able-bodied man is a soldier or a sailor, every child is a scout, and every woman a nurse or a munition worker. We are anxious to waste our resources on preparedness rather than on the education of the young. We hanker for the greatest navy in the world at a cost of several billions of dollars. We aspire after a million headed, billion armed navy and army. We clamor for universal, compulsory, military service in which our children should be drilled for murder and slaughter at the decree of a few autocratic officials and officers. We imitate Europe slavishly, in spite of the fact that the policy of preparedness or of "armed peace" has kept Europe in a state of turmoil for generations, has brought her to the brink of ruin, and has plunged her into the most cruel and most destructive war ever waged by man.

The recent estimate of Count von Roedern, Secretary of the Imperial German Treasury, puts the total cost of the war to date, the end of 1916, for all the belligerents, at fifty-nine and a half billions of dollars. The Mechanics and Metals National Bank of New York City figures that seventy-five billion dollars will be spent for direct military purposes, if the war lasts another year. The enormity of that expenditure can only be realized if we consider that the total wealth of Great Britain and Ireland is eighty-five billions of dollars, that of Germany eighty billions, that of France fifty billions, that of Russia forty billions, that of Austria-Hungary twenty-five billions, and that of Italy twenty billions. Such waste is appalling.

According to the figures given by Mr. Frank H. Simonds, eighteen and a half million casualties, of which deaths make up nearly one-quarter, is the toll already levied on the fighting men of all the belligerent nations by twenty-six months of war. More than any other war the present European struggle squanders the wealth of empires and sacrifices the lives of nations.

Our social status is a reversion to savagery of the most degenerate type, an atavistic lapse towards the paleolithic and neolithic man, only more brutal, on account of the greater power for evil possessed by modern man. What Hun or Vandal ever dreamt of such colossal destruction! The fame of Attila, Jenghiz Khan, Batu, and Tamerlane pales and fades before the glory of' the Kaiser. In a couple of years the aggressive German "Kultur" has caused more ruin to humanity than all the invasions of the yellow peril in the history of mankind. Can we take issue with the late Professor Royce of Harvard when he declares the German Empire to be "the willful and the deliberate enemy of the human race"?

Some future historian in describing our times will place us below the moral level of our contemporaries, the Bushman and the Hottentot. He may say: "Towards the end of the nineteenth and at the beginning of the twentieth century there took place a vast accumulation of wealth, due to a rapid development of science and practical arts. Instead, however, of improving their condition, European nations deteriorated morally and intellectually.

"Liberal education gave way to technical training. Science served greed. Education became mechanical and military in character. The successful banker, the greedy usurer, the commonplace storekeeper, the mediocre shopkeeper, the philistine patriotic business man became the patterns, the ideals, the guides, and leaders of commercialized nations. Advertising and notoriety became the rage and the bane of society". The thinker gave way to the tinker, the scientist to the mechanic, the artist to the artisan, the genius to the philistine. False patriotism of the jingo type, controlled and animated by industrial and commercial interests, became the standard of nations. An insane frenzy of militarism seized on the minds of nations. Blind obedience became a virtue.

"The state enslaved the individual. Drill and discipline stupefied people. Nations boasting of scientific efficiency and 'kultur' broke treaties, attacked, destroyed, deported, enslaved whole populations of small, weak, neighboring countries. Women and babes were drowned like rats in the middle of the ocean. Aeroplanes and Zeppelins showered explosive missiles on defenceless people. For such cowardly, inhuman, and diabolical acts the miscreants were decorated and honored as heroes by their alleged superiors. Man could not have fallen to any lower level.

"The elements of nature were let loose for the ruin of nations. Man gloried in his devilish, military, inventive power of destruction. Professors, carrying high the banner of 'kultur,' exulted in the degrading, vicious process of training by which the individual is hypnotized and narcotized into submission to a brutal organization of military junkers, hallowed by the name of State. All conception of free, individual development was lost among the Germanic tribes of Central Europe. It was the darkest period in the history of mankind. Assaults on countries, massacres of nations, deportation of populations into slavery for powerful munition interests, all such outrages, dignified by the name of war for the defense of the Fatherland, had not their parallel even in the most degrading period of the history of humanity. Man was crazed with the lust of blood, frenzied with rapine and slaughter."

Such will be the just estimate of our times by a future impartial historian.

We possess indeed vast stores of wealth, but we have not as yet learned their use. Like silly upstarts, we use our wealth for dissipation and ruin. Our greed and cruelty seem to grow with our possessions. Greed with its army and navy is like the Biblical horseleech that "hath two daughters crying, 'Give, give.'" Human life, man's genius, we hold in no esteem. We sink the value of man in the price of his product. We raise the value of stock, but lower the worth of man. Our young generation is trained by fear into discipline and obedience. We suppress the genius in the child, raise mediocrity, and cultivate the philistine.

"Obedience and discipline arc the mainstay of family and school," told me an otherwise intelligent schoolmaster. "I control my children with kindness, if possible, and if needs be, with force." The child is trained to act not by the light of reason, but by the command of superior force. The child is ruled by fear!

As a protection against fear the child learns to be secretive, evasive of truth, and cowardly of action. These traits of character, acquired in early childhood, become basic. The child will never fully rid himself of fear and its distressing consequences. Fear will stay with him, and dog his steps all his life long.

Fear is one of the most fundamental of animal instincts, it is the companion of the most primitive impulse of self-preservation. Once this fear instinct is aroused, it grows like an avalanche in its downward course. In later life this fear instinct becomes manifested in various ways, giving rise to the most distressing nervous and mental symptoms. In my medical practice, as specialist of nervous and mental diseases, I have traced again and again the worst forms of maladies to the fear instinct aroused in early childhood.

Training by fear, submission, and obedience opens the door wide to all kinds of nervous and mental germs, weakening the mental and moral constitution of man. Man becomes unreasonable, capricious, driven by the impulse of self-preservation, and by the furies of the fear instinct. The impulse of self-preservation with its satellite the fear instinct becomes predominant in character which lacks the stamina of sturdiness, frankness, open-mindedness and independence.

A person brought up in the school of fear and blind obedience lacks steadiness of purpose, courage, independence, critical judgment, becomes bigoted and intolerant. He falls an easy prey to the suggestions of his times and surroundings, succumbs to the influence of unscrupulous leaders. Such a person lacks mental and moral poise, he is wanting in the true courage of reason, present in the

fully developed man and woman. He can not with-
stand the pressure of social opinion, being unable to
stand by his post in the face of threatening social
opposition. Ruled by fear at home, he is governed
by terror in society. He is afraid of social punish-
ment, "of losing face," as the Chinese say, with his
neighbors, gossips, circles and clubs. He dreads
above all the judgment of the crowd, and is scared
by the jeers and ridicule of the mob. Human life interests become limited by the narrow horizon of a
mob-ruled personality. The unceasing obedience to
the suggestions of the crowd weakens and loosens
the reasoning and moral fibre, reduces the energies
of the mind to the animal level, controlled by self-
preservation and fear.

With reduced and impoverished energies, the
person, in case of trouble and misfortune, is unable
to fall back on his inner resources, he falls a prey to
worry, fear, anxiety, and disease. In other cases the
intellectual and moral powers are enfeebled by the
rigid discipline and by the course of enforced obedience, the person falls a victim to all forms of
temptations. With no principle to guide him, with
no will to stay him, the person drifts helplessly on
the stream of life. Lured by seductive sirens, his life
is finally wrecked on the rocks and reefs of vice,
sin, crime, and disease.

Where stumbling on vice, disease, and crime is
avoided, the person inevitably lands on the dull

shores of the Lotophagi. Ideas and ideals are forgotten and forsaken in the routine of animal existence. This is the land of Philistinism, a land where all human, humane interests, independent thought, and courageous action are wanting. Philistines are uncritical, unconscious of defects and faults, living in the mire of self-contented stupidity and mediocrity. They cease to grow mentally and morally. Their intellectual and moral capacities become paralyzed, atrophied. Man becomes the equal of the brute.

With a philistine education and training, man is fit to become one of those unfortunate and pitiful European pawns and automata who obey blindly the commands of their superior officers. Philistines shoot, stab, poison, pillage, burn, outrage, and murder at the command of unscrupulous, self-seeking leaders, brutal junkers, bloodhounds of empires.

Brought up in a school of fear, obedience, and suggestibility, the philistine, like Cain, murders his brother without aim and without understanding the full significance of the awful deed. He is no more responsible than is the machine gun which he accurately trains and points at his supposed enemies. Philistines are led to the battlefield like cattle to the slaughter house. Philistines have no personality, no individuality, they are cogs in wheels, links in chains of monster mechanisms.

The philistine, the product of our home and school" is suggestible and gullible, he is always on the lookout for authority, for a leader whom he should worship, by whose opinions and conviction he is ready to swear, whose command he is ready and proud to follow. The philistine is good material for mobs, for mental epidemics, for religious crazes, and for all kinds of hysterical movements in which not reason but emotional automatism is in the foreground. *Philistinism, stupidity, and implicit obedience of a monstrous, efficient war machine are intimately interrelated. The individual becomes a private, the nation an army, and the country a camp.*

Do we as parents wish to bring up our children as soulless, willless machines? Do we wish them to be without good judgment, without personal convictions? Do we wish them to be led about like cattle? We certainly wish them to be of strong nature and sturdy character, able to stand by their convictions, able to use their critical judgment, able to discriminate the right from the wrong, able to love the good and avoid the evil.

In The *Psychology of Suggestion*, published by me in 1897, I arrive at the conclusion that "Personality is suppressed by the rigidity of social organization; the cultivated, civilized individual is an automaton, a mere puppet. . . Again, "Under the enormous weight of the sociostatic press. . . the personal self sinks, the suggestible, subconscious, social, impersonal self rises to the surface, gets trained and cultivated, and becomes the hysterical actor in all the tragedies of historical life." . . . In recent European events the suggestible, social self plays the chief rôle.

In the same work I come to the following conclusion: "When social conditions are of such a nature as to charge society with strong emotional excitement, or when institutions dwarf individuality, when they arrest personal growth, when they hinder the free development and exercise of the personal, controlling consciousness, then society falls into a hypnoid condition, the social mind gets disaggregated. The gregarious self begins to move within the bosom of the crowd, and becomes active the demon of the demos emerges to the surface of social life, and throws the body politic into convulsions of demoniac fury."

The European horrors, atrocities, and brutalities, dignified by the stupefying and hypnotizing slogan "Kultur, Patriotism," are due to the early training, by fear and force, of the individual into submission to superior authority. Such pernicious training sacrifices the genius of the child, the originality of the man, to a highly efficient, but brutal and bloodthirsty Moloch State. The European war is a mental plague which attacks gigantic, social aggregates when their ultimate constituent units, the individuals, are deprived of independent thought and liberty of decision and action, when men are swayed by hypnotizing suggestions of "superior leaders" who represent the interests not of every individual at his best, but of high noble castes and of commercial classes. The organized murder of European nations is due to the stifling of human genius by the cultivation of mob spirit which is the cause of all forms of social insanity and mental epidemics.

In the stifling of the genius of the child and the cultivation of the mob spirit America does not lag behind Europe. Mental epidemics, excited by the fear instinct and by the impulse of self-preservation, are prevalent in the States. As described by me in *The Psychology of Suggestion*: "American society oscillates between acute financial mania and attacks of religious insanity. No sooner is the business fever over than the delirium acutum of religious mania sets in. Society is thrown from Scylla into Charybdis. From the heights of financial speculation society sinks into the abyss of revivalism. American society seems to *suffer from circular insanity*."

Revivalism, a mental frenzy to which the American mob mind is specially prone, is a resurrection of Greek Bacchanalia and Roman Saturnalia. Revivals are emotional debauches, religious orgies. As I had pointed out in the same work: "Revivalism is far more dangerous to the life of society than drunkenness... As a sot man falls below the brute; as a revivalist he sinks lower than the sot."

If Europe is in violent convulsions of war insanity, America suffers from no less serious mental maladies,—speculation frenzies, revival manias, and preparedness plagues. Mental epidemics are ineradicable afflictions of the highly evolved mob spirit characteristic of the philistine. The evolution of the philistine is the involution of genius. Philistinism is social decay. *The progress of humanity is from brute to man, from Philistine to Genius.*

Boris Sidis
Sidis Institute
Maplewood Farm,
Portsmouth, New Hampshire

CHAPTER ONE

I ADDRESS myself to you, fathers and mothers, and to you, open-minded readers. I take it for granted that your lifework is with you a serious matter and that you put forth all your efforts to do your best in the walk of life which you have chosen. I assume that you want to develop your energies to the highest efficiency and bring out the best there is in you. I assume that you earnestly wish and strive to bring out and develop to the highest efficiency the faculties not only of your children, but also those of your friends and co-workers with whom you associate in your daily vocation, and that you are deeply interested in the education of your countrymen and their children, who share with you the duties, rights and privileges of citizenship. I also assume that as men and women of liberal education you are not limited to the narrow interests of one particular subject, to the exclusion of all else. I assume that you are especially interested in the development of personality as a whole, the true aim of education. I also assume that you realize that what is requisite is not some more routine, not more desiccated, quasi-scientific methods of educational psychology, not the sawdust of college-pseudogogics and philistine, normal school-training, but more light on the problems of life. What you want is not the training of philistines, but the education of genius.

We need more light, more information on "the problems of life." Is it not too big a phrase to employ? On a second thought, however, I must say that your problems are the problems of life. For the problems of education are fundamental, they are at the bottom of all vital problems. The ancient Greeks were aware of it and paid special attention to education. In rearing his revolutionary, utopian edifice, Plato insists on education as the foundation of a new social, moral and intellectual life. Plato in his Republic makes Socrates tell his interlocutor, Adeimantus: "Then you are aware that in every work the beginning is the most important part, especially in dealing with anything young and tender? For that is the time when any impression which one may desire to communicate is most readily stamped and taken."

We may say that all man's struggles, religious, moral and economical, all the combats and conflicts that fill the history of mankind, can be traced finally to the nature and vigor of the desires, beliefs and strivings which have been cultivated by the social environment in the early life of the individual. The character of a nation is moulded by the nature of its education. The character of society depends on the early training of its constituent units. The fatalism, the submissiveness of the Oriental; the aestheticism, the independence, love of innovations and inquisitiveness of the ancient Greek; the ruggedness, sturdiness, harshness and conservatism of the ancient Roman; the emotionalism, the religious fervor of the ancient Hebrew; the commercialism, restlessness, speculation and scientific spirit of modern times, are all the results of the nature of the early education the individual gets in his respective social environment. We may say that the education of early life forms the very foundation of the social structure.

Like clay in the hands of the potter, so is man in the hands of his community. Society fashions the beliefs, the desires, the aims, the strivings, the knowledge, the ideals, the character, the minds, the very selves of its constituent units. Who has the control of this vital function of moulding minds? Fathers and mothers, the child is under your control. To your hands, to your care is entrusted the fate of young generations, the fate of the future community, which, consciously or unconsciously, you fashion according to the accepted standards and traditions with which you have been imbued in your own education.

It is related, I think, in Plutarch's Lives, of Themistocles telling with the ironical frankness characteristic of the Greek temperament that his son possessed the greatest power in Greece: "For the Athenians command the rest of Greece, I command the Athenians, his mother commands me, and he commands his mother." This bit of Greek irony is not without its significance. The mind of the growing generation controls the future of nations. The boy is father to the man, as the proverb has it; he controls the future. But who controls the boy? The home, the mother and father, the guides of the child's early life. For it is in early life that the foundation of our mental edifice is laid. All that is good, valid and solid in man's mental structure depends on the breadth, width, depth, and solidity of that foundation.

CHAPTER TWO

THAT the groundwork of man's character is laid in his childhood appears as a trivial platitude. I am almost ashamed to bring it before you. And yet, as I look round me and find how apt we are to forget this simple precept which is so fundamental in our life, I cannot help calling your attention to it. If we consider the matter, we can well understand the reason why its full significance is not realized. We must remember that all science begins with axioms which are apparently truisms. What is more of a truism than the axioms of Geometry and Mechanics—that the whole is greater than the part, that things which are equal to the same thing are equal to one another, or that a body remains in the same state unless an external force changes it? And yet the whole of Mathematics and Mechanics is built on those simple axioms.

The elements of science are just such obvious platitudes. What is needed is to use them as efficient tools and by their means draw the consequent effects. The same holds true in the science of education. The axiom or the law of early training is not new, it is well known, but it is unfortunately too often neglected and forgotten, and its significance is almost completely lost.

It is certainly surprising how this law of early training is so disregarded, so totally ignored in the education of the child. Not only do we neglect to lay the necessary solid basis in the early life of the child, a solid basis ready for the future structure, we do not even take care to clear the ground. In fact, we even make the child's soul a dunghill, full of vermin of superstitions, fears and prejudices, a hideous heap saturated with the spirit of credulity.

We regard the child's mind as a *tabula rasa*, a vacant lot, and empty on it all our rubbish and refuse. We labor under the delusion that stories and fairy tales, myths and deceptions about life and man are good for the child's mind. Is it a wonder that on such a foundation men can only put up shacks and shanties? We forget the simple fact that what is harmful for the adult is still more harmful to the child. Surely what is poisonous to the grown-up mind cannot be useful food to the young. If credulity in old wives' tales, lack of individuality, sheepish submissiveness, barrack-discipline, unquestioned and uncritical belief in authority, meaningless imitation of jingles and gibberish, memorization of mother-goose wisdom, repetition of incomprehensible prayers and articles of creed, unintelligent aping of good manners, silly games, prejudices and superstitions and fears of the supernormal and supernatural, are censured in adults, why 'should we approve their cultivation in the young?

At home and at school we drill into the child's mind uncritical beliefs in stories and tales, fictions and figments, fables and myths, creeds and dogmas which poison the very sources of the child's mind. At home and at school we give the child over as a prey to all sorts of fatal germs of mental diseases and moral depravity. We leave the child's mind an open field to be sown with dragon's teeth which bring forth a whole crop of pernicious tendencies,—love and admiration of successful evil, and adoration of the rule of brute force. From the dragon's teeth sown in early childhood there rises in later life a whole brood of flint-hearted men who blindly jostle and fight and mercilessly tear one another, to obtain for some greedy Jason, some witch of a Medea their coveted golden fleece.

CHAPTER THREE

W E regard with disapproval the bloody combats of some savage tribe; we regard with horror the sacrifice of children and prisoners to some idol of a Phoenician Moloch or Mexican Huitzlio-Potchli; we are shocked at the criminal proceedings of the infamous Torquemada with his inquisition glorying in its terrors and tortures in the name of Christ; we are sickened as we read of the religious wars in Europe; we shudder at the horrors of the night of St. Bartholomew; we are appalled by the recent slaughters of the Jews in Russia, by the wholesale massacre of the Christians in Turkey.

All such atrocities, we say, belong to barbaric ages and are only committed in semi-civilized countries. We flatter ourselves that we are different in this age of enlightenment and civilization. Are we different? Have we changed? Have we a right to fling stones at our older brothers, the savage and the barbarian? We are so used to our life that we do not notice its evils and misery. We can easily see the mote in the eye of our neighbor, but do not notice the beam in our own.

We are still savage at heart. Our civilization is mere gloss, a thin coating of paint and varnish. Our methods of inflicting pain are more refined than those of the Indian, but no less cruel, while the number of the victims sacrificed to our greed and rapacity may even exceed the numbers fallen by the sword of the barbarian or by the torch of the fanatic. The slums in our cities are foul and filthy, teeming with deadly germs of disease where the mortality of our infants and children in some cases rises to the frightful figure of 204 per thousand!

The sanitary conditions of our cities are filthy and deadly. They carry in their wake all forms of plagues, pests and diseases, among which tuberculosis is so well known to the laity. "Tuberculosis," reads a report of a Tenement House Commission, "is one of the results of our inhumane tenements; it follows in the train of our inhumane sweatshops. It comes where the hours of labor are long and the wages are small; it afflicts the children who are sent to labor when they should yet be in school."

"The Consumers' League," says Mr. John Graham Brooks, "long hesitated to lay stress upon these aspects of filth and disease, because of their alarmist and sensational nature, and of the immediate and grave risk to the consumer of the goods manufactured in the sweatshop and the tenement house. If the sweatshop spread diphtheria and scarlet fever, there is the hue and cry before personal danger. But these diseases are the very slightest elements of the real risk to the general good. It is the spoiled human life, with its deadly legacy of enfeebled mind and body, that reacts directly and indirectly on the social whole." We do not realize that we drift into national degeneracy. We fail to realize that we raise a generation of stunted lives, of physical and nervous wrecks, of mental invalids and moral cripples.

We boast of our wealth unrivalled by other countries and by former ages. We should remember the great poverty of our masses, the filthy conditions of our wealthy cities, with their loathsome city-slums, in which human beings live, breed and teem like so many worms.

We spend on barracks and prisons more than we do on schools and colleges. What is the level of a civilization in which the cost of crime and war far exceeds that of the education of its future citizens? We spend on our army and navy a quarter of a billion dollars, which is found to be insufficient, while the "total money burden of crime amounts in this country to the enormous sum of 600 million dollars a year!"

The cost of crime alone is so enormous that a representative of the Board of Charities of one of our Eastern states considers "the entire abolition of all the penal codes and the complete liberty of the criminal class." Our civilization can boast of the city-slum, the abode of misery and crime, the gift of our modern industrial progress, wealth and prosperity.

Professor James and myself were over once on a visit to a charitable institution for mentally defective. With his clear eye for the incongruities and absurdities of life, Professor James remarked to me that idiots and imbeciles were given the comforts, in fact, the luxuries of life, while healthy children, able boys and girls, had to struggle for a livelihood. Children under fourteen work in factories, work at a wage of about twenty-five cents a day, and, according to the labor bureau, the daily wage of the factory children of the South is often as low as fifteen cents and sometimes falls to nine cents. In many of our colleges many a student has to live on the verge of starvation, freeze in a summer overcoat the whole winter and warm his room by burning newspapers in the grate. We are charitable and help our mediocrities, imbeciles and idiots, while we neglect our talent and genius. We have a blind faith that genius, like murder, will out. We know of successful talent, but we do not know of the great amount of unsuccessful talent and genius that has gone to waste. We favor imbecility and slight genius.

One of the physicians of the institution overheard our conversation and attempted to justify his work by an argument commonly advanced and uncritically accepted—"Our civilization, our Christian civilization values human life." Does our civilization really value human life? The infant mortality of the slums of our large cities and the factory work of our young children do not seem to justify such a claim.

The loss of life on our railways is as large as one caused by a national war. Thus the number of persons killed on America on railways during a period of three years ending June 30, 1900, was about 22,000, while the mortality of British forces, including death from disease, during three years of the South African war amounted to 22,000. In 1901, one out of every 400 railway employees was killed and one out of every 26 was injured. In 1902, 2,969 employees were killed and 50,524 were injured.

Commenting on the statistics of railway accidents, Mr. John Graham Brooks says: "One has to read and re-read these figures before their gruesome significance is in the least clear. If we add the mining, iron and lumbering industries,—portions of which are more dangerous than the railroad,—some conception is possible of the mutilated life due to machinery as it is now run." It may also be of interest to learn that, according to the calculation made by a representative of one of the insurance companies, more than a million and a half are annually killed and injured in the United States alone.

The waste of human life is in fact greater than in any previous age. "Saul hath slain his thousands, but David his ten thousands." Think of our modern warfare, with its infernal machines of carnage, mowing down more men in a day than the warlike Assyrians and Romans, with their crude bows, arrows and catapults, could destroy in a century. And is not our country, our civilized Christian society, with its high valuation of human life, keeping on increasing its army and navy, and perfecting deadly weapons of slaughter and carnage? What about the justice dealt out by Judge Lynch? From 1882 to 1900 there were about three thousand lynchings! What about our grand imperial policy? What about our dominance over weak and ignorant tribes, treated in no gentle way by the armed fist of their civilized masters, who send to the benighted heathens their missionaries to preach religion and their soldiers to enforce the sale of narcotics and other civilizing goods?

CHAPTER FOUR

WE are stock-blind to our own barbarities; we do not realize the enormities of our life and consider our age and country as civilized and enlightened. We censure the faults of other societies, but do not notice our own. Thus Lecky, in describing Roman society, says: "The gladiatorial games form indeed the one feature which to a modern mind is most inconceivable in its atrocity. That not only men, but women, man advanced period of civilization,—men and women who not only professed, but very frequently acted upon a high code of morals—should have made the carnage of men their habitual amusement, that all this should have continued for centuries with scarcely a protest, is one of the most startling facts in moral history. It is, however, perfectly normal, while it opens out fields of ethical inquiry of a very deep, though painful, character."

As in modern times, our college authorities justify the brutalities of football and prize-fights, so in ancient times the great moralists of those ages justified their gladiatorial games. Thus the great orator, the moralizing philosopher, Cicero, in speaking of the gladiatorial games, tells us: "When guilty men are compelled to fight, no better discipline against suffering and death can be presented to the eye." And it is certainly instructive for us to learn that "the very men who looked down with delight, when tile sand of the arena reddened with human blood, made the theater ring with applause when Terence in his famous line proclaimed the brotherhood of men."

One feeble protest is on record, a protest coming from the mother of civilization, from ancient Athens. "When an attempt was made to introduce the games into Athens, the philosopher Demonax appealed successfully to the better feelings of the people by exclaiming: "You must first overthrow the altar of pity ! »

The philosopher Demonax had not the compromising spirit of the modern professor. Although the brutal games of our youth and populace need a Demonax, we certainly should not look for one in our colleges and universities. Our college authorities assure us that athletic prestige is indispensable to a good university. In fact, according to some official statements, football teams are supposed to express the superior intellectual activities of our foremost colleges. Like Cicero of old, we claim that "our games are good,—they train men, and no better discipline can be presented to the eye."

The fact is, man is bat-blind to the evils of the environment in which he is bred. He takes those evils as a matter of course, and even finds good reasons to justify them as edifying and elevating. In relation to his own surroundings, man is in the primitive condition of the Biblical Adam,—he is not conscious of his own moral nakedness. Six days in the week we witness and uphold the wholesale carnage, national and international, political, economical, in shops, factories, mines, railroads and on the battlefields, while on the seventh we sing hymns to the God of mercy, love and peace.

We pick up the first newspapers or popular magazines that come to our hand, and we read of wars, slaughters, murders, lynchings, crimes and outrages on life and liberty; we read of strikes, lockouts, of tales of starvation and of frightful infant mortality; we read of diseases and epidemics ravaging the homes of our working population; we read of corporation iniquities, of frauds and corruption of our legislative bodies, of the control of polities by the criminal classes of the great metropolis of our land. We read of all that evil and corruption, but forget them next moment.

Our social life is corrupt, our body politic is eaten through with cankers and sores, "the whole head is sick and the whole heart is faint. From the sole of the foot even unto the head, there is no soundness in it; but wounds, and bruises and putre-fying sores, and yet we think we are a civilized peo-ple, superior to all countries and to all ages. "The voice of our brother's blood crieth unto us from the ground." How can we be so callous? How can we be so mole-blind and so stone-deaf?

The truth is, we have but a thin varnish of hu-maneness, glossing over a rude barbarism. With our lips we praise the God of love, but in our hearts we adore the God of force. flow much physical force is worshipped we can realize from the crowds that throng the games of base-ball, football, prize-fights and boxing exhibitions. They go into tens of thou-sands. flow many would be drawn by a St. Paul, an Epictetus, or a Socrates?

The newspaper, the mirror of our social life, is filled with the names and exploits of our magnates of high finance, our money-mongers and usurers. Our journals teem with deeds and scandals of our refined "smart set" set up as patterns, as ideals, after which our middle class so longingly craves. Like the Israelites of old we worship golden calves and sacred bulls. Our daughters yearn after the barbaric shimmer and glitter of the bejewelled, bespangled, empty-minded, parasitic females of "the smart set." Our college boys admire the feats of the trained athlete and scorn the work of the "grind." Our very schoolboys crave for the fame of a Jeffries and a Johnson. If in the depths of space there is some solar system inhabited by really rational beings, and if one of such beings should by some miracle happen to visit our planet, he would no doubt turn away in horror.

CHAPTER FIVE

We press our children into the triumphant march of our industrial juggernaut. Over 1,700,000 children under 15 years of age toil in fields, factories, mines and workshops. The slums and the factory cripple the energies of our young generation The slaughter of the innocents and the sacrifice of our children to the insatiable Moloch of industry exclude us from the rank of civilized society and place us on the level of barbaric nations.

Our educators are narrow-minded pedants. They are occupied with the dry bones of text-books, the sawdust of pedagogics and the would-be scientific experiments of educational psychology; they are ignorant of the real vital problems of human interests, a knowledge of which goes to make the truly educated man.

About the middle of the nineteenth century, Buckle made the prediction that no war was any more to occur among civilized nations. Henceforth peace was to reign supreme. "The wolf shall dwell with the lamb, and the leopard shall lie down with the kid; their young ones shall lie down together, and the lion shall eat straw like the ox. . . . Nations shall beat their swords into ploughshares and their spears into pruning hooks. Nation shall not lift lip sword against nation, nor shall they learn war any more." This prophecy was rather hasty. We have had since the Civil war, the Franco-Prussian war, tile Spanish-American war, the Boer war, the Russo-Japanese war, not counting the ceaseless wars of extermination carried on by civilized nations among the various semi-civilized nations and primitive tribes. Civilized nations do not as yet beat their swords into ploughshares, but keep on increasing the strength of their "armed peace," and are ready to fight bloody battles in the quest of new lands and the conquest of new markets.

In spite of The Hague conference of peace convoked by the peace-loving Czar, no other age has had such large standing armies provided with such costly and efficient weapons of execution ready for instant use. The red spectre still stalks abroad claiming its victims. We still believe in the baptism of fire and redemption by blood. The dogma of blood-redemption is still at the basis of our faith and, consciously or unconsciously, we brand that sacred creed on the minds of the young generation. We are not educated to see and understand the wretchedness, the misery of our life,-the evil of the world falls on the blind spot of our eye. In the name of evolution and the survival of the fittest, we justify the grasping arm of the strong, and even glory in the extermination of the weak. The weak, we say, must be weeded out by the processes of natural selection. The strong are the best; it is right that they should survive and flourish like a green bay tree. The fact is that we are still dominated by the law of the jungle, the den and the cave. We are still wild at heart. We still harken to the call of the wild; we are ruled by the fist, the claw and the tooth.

Love, justice, gentleness, peace, reason, sympathy and pity, all humane feelings and promptings are with us sentiments of unnatural" or supernatural religion which we profess in our churches, but in which we really have no faith as good for actual life. We mistake brutishness for courage, and by fight and by war we train the beast in man.

All humane feelings are regarded as so many hindrances to progress; they favor, we claim, the survival of the weak. We are, of course, evolutionists, and believe most firmly in progress. We believe that the luxuries and vices of the strong are conducive to prosperity, and that the evils of life by the automatic grinding of that grind-organ known as the process of evolution *somehow* lead to a higher civilization.

When in the beginning of the eighteenth century Bernard de Mandeville proclaimed the apparently paradoxical principle that *Private Vices are Public Benefits*, the academic moralists were shocked at such profane brutality. Mandeville only proclaimed the leading, the guiding principle of the coming age of industrial prosperity. We now know better. Are we not evolutionists? Have we not learned that progress and evolution and the improvement of the race are brought about by the fierce struggle for existence, by the process of natural selection, by the merciless elimination of the weak and by the triumph of the strong and the fit? What is the use of being sentimental? Like Brennus, the Gaul, we throw our sword on the scales of blinded justice and shout triumphantly "*Væ victis*!"

CHAPTER SIX

WE are confirmed optimists and sow optimism broadcast. We have optimistic clubs and mental scientists and Christian scientists,—all afflicted with incurable ophthalmia to surrounding evil and misery. We are scientific, we are evolutionists, we have faith in the sort of optimism taught by Leibnitz in bis famous Theodicea. We are the Candides of our oracles, the Panglosses. You may possibly remember what Voltaire writes of Professor Pangloss. "Pangloss used to teach the science of metaphysico-theologo-cosmologo-noodle-ology. He demonstrated to admiration that there is no effect without a cause and that this is the best of all possible worlds. It has been proved, said Pangloss, that things cannot be otherwise than they are; for everything, the end for which everything is made, is necessarily the best end. Observe how noses are made to carry 'spectacles, and spectacles we have accordingly. Everything that is, is the best that could possibly be." It is such shallow optimism that now gains currency.

Verily, we are afflicted with mental cataract. "If we should bring clearly to a man's sight," says Schopenhauer, "the terrible sufferings and miseries to which his life is constantly exposed, he would be seized with horror, and if we were to conduct the confirmed optimist through the hospitals, infirmaries, and surgical operating-rooms, through prisons, asylums, torture-chambers and slave-kennels, over battlefields and places of execution; if we were to open to him all the dark abodes of misery, where it hides itself from the glance of cold curiosity, he would understand at last the nature of this best of possible worlds."

Schopenhauer is metaphysical, pessimistic, but he is certainly not blinded by a shallow optimism to the realities of life. Drunk with the spirit of optimism, we do not realize the degradation, the misery and poverty of our life. Meanwhile the human genius, the genius which all of us possess, languishes, famishes, and perishes, while the brute alone emerges in triumph. We are so overcome by the faith in the transcendent, optimistic evolution of the good, that through the misty heavenly, angelic visions, we do not discern the cloven hoof of the devil.

Professor James in a recent address told the Radcliffe graduates that the aim of a college-education is "to recognize the good man," when you see him. This advice may be good for Radcliffe young ladies; but, fathers and mothers, the true education of life is the recognition of evil wherever it is met.

The Bible begins the story of man in a paradise of ignorance and finishes it with his tasting of the fruits of the forbidden tree of knowledge of good and evil. "And the eyes of them both were opened and they knew that they were naked. And the Lord God said,—Behold, the man is become as one of us to know good and evil, and now, lest he put forth his hand and take also of the tree of life and eat and live for ever. Therefore, the Lord God sent him forth from the garden of Eden. So he drove out the man." We prefer the sinful, mortal, but godlike man with his knowledge of evil to the brutish phlilistine in the bliss of Elysium.

CHAPTER SEVEN

I N the education of the young generation the purpose of the nation is to bring up the child as a good man, as a liberal-minded citizen, devoted soul and body to the interests of social welfare. This purpose in the education of the young citizen is of the utmost importance in every society, but it is a vital need in a democratic society. We do not want narrow-minded patriots devoted to party-factions, nor bigoted sectarians, nor greedy entrepreneurs fastening in trusts, like so many barnacles, on the body-politic. We do not want ringleaders and mobs, unscrupulous bosses and easily led voters. What we need is men having at heart the welfare of their fellow-men.

The purpose of the education provided by the nation for its young generation is the rearing of healthy, talented, broad-minded citizens. "We need, above all, good citizens, active and intelligent, with a knowledge of life and with a delicate sense of discrimination and detection of evil in all its protean forms; we need strong-minded citizens with grit and courage to resist oppression and root out evil wherever it is found. A strong sense of recognition of evil should be the social sense of every well-educated citizen as a safeguard of social and national life. The principle of recognition of evil under all its guises is at the basis of the true education of man.

Is it not strange that this vital principle of education, the recognition of evil,—a fundamental principle with the great thinkers of humanity,—should remain so sadly neglected by our educators and public instructors? Our educators are owl-wise, our teachers are pedants and all their ambition is the turning out of smooth, well-polished philistines. It is a sad case of the blind leading the blind.

It is certainly unfortunate that the favored type of superintendent of our public education should be such a hopeless philistine, possessed of all the conceit of the mediocre business man. Routine is his ideal. Originality and genius are spurned and suppressed. Our school-superintendent with his well-organized training-shop is proud of the fact that there is no place for genius in our schools.

Unfortunate and degraded is the nation that has

handed over its childhood and youth to guidance and control by hide-bound mediocrity. Our school-managers are respected by the laity as great educators and are looked up to by the teachers as able business men. Their merit is routine, discipline and the hiring of cheap teaching-employees.

It is certainly a great misfortune to the nation that a good number of our would-be scientific pedagogues are such mediocrities, with so absurd an exaggeration of their importance that they are well satisfied if the mass of their pupils turn out exact reproductions of the silly pedagogue. What can be expected of a nation that entrusts the fate of its young generation to the care or carelessness of young girls, to the ire of old maids, and to pettifogging officials with their educational red tape, discipline and routine,—petty bureaucrats animated with a hatred towards talent and genius?

The goody-goody schoolma'am, the mandarin-schoolmaster, the philistine-pedagogue, the pedant-administrator with his business capacities, have proved themselves incompetent to deal with the education of the young. They stifle talent, they stupefy the intellect, they paralyze the will, they suppress genius, they benumb the faculties of our children. The educator, with his pseudo-scientific, pseudo-psychological pseudogogics, can only bring up a set of philistines with firm, set habits,—marionettes,—dolls.

Business is put above learning, administration above education, discipline and order above cultivation of genius and talent. Our schools and colleges are controlled by business men. The school-boards, the boards of trustees of almost every school and college ill the country consist mainly of, manufacturers, store-keepers, tradesmen, bulls and bears of Wall street and the market-place. What wonder that they bring with them the ideals and methods of the factory, the store, the bank and the saloon. If the saloon controls politics, the shop controls education.

Business men are no more competent to run schools and colleges than astronomers are fit to run hotels and theaters. Our whole educational system is vicious. A popular scientific journal entered a protest against the vulgarization of our colleges, the department-store trade methods of our universities, but to no avail. The popular hero, the administrative business superintendent still holds sway, and poisons the sources of our social life by debasing the very foundation of our national education.

CHAPTER EIGHT

F ROM time to time the "educational" methods
of our philistine teachers are brought to light.
A girl is forced by a schoolma'am of one of our
large cities to stay in a corner for hours, because she
unintentionally transgressed against the barrack-
discipline of the school-regulations. When the parents became afraid of the girl's health and naturally
took her out of school, the little girl was dragged
before the court by the truant officer. Fortunately
"the judge turned to the truant officer and asked
him how the girl could be a truant, if she had been
suspended. He didn't believe in breaking children's
wills."

In another city a pupil of genius was excluded
from school because "he did not fall in with the system" laid out by the "very able business-superinten-

dent." A schoolmistress conceives the happy idea of converting two of her refractory pupils into pincushions for the edification of her class. An "educational" administrative superintendent of a large, prosperous community told a lady who brought to him her son, an extraordinarily able boy, "I shall not take your boy. into my high-school, in spite of his knowledge." When the mother asked him to listen to her, he lost patience and told her with all the force of his school-authority, "Madam, put a rope around his neck, weigh him well down with bricks!"

A principal of a high school in one of the prominent New England towns dismisses a highly talented pupil because, to quote verbatim from the original school document, "He is not amenable to the discipline of the school, as his school life has been too short to establish him in the habit' of obedience." "His intellect," the principal's official letter goes on to say, "remains a marvel to us, but we do not feel, and in this I think I speak for all, that he is in the right place." In other words, in the opinion of those remarkable pedagogues, educators and teachers, the school is not the right place for talent and genius!

A superintendent of schools in lecturing before an audience of "subordinate teachers" told them emphatically that there was no place for genius in our schools. Dear old fogies, one can well understand your indignation! Here we have worked out some fine methods, clever rules, beautiful systems and then comes genius and upsets the whole structure! It is a shame! Genius cannot fit into the pigeon-holes of the office desk. Choke genius, and things will move smoothly in the school and the office.

Not long ago we were informed by one of those successful college-mandarins, lionized by office-clerks, superintendents and tradesmen, that he could measure education by the foot-rule! Our Regents are supposed to raise the level of education by a vicious system of examination and coaching, a system which Professor James, in a private conversation with me, has aptly characterized as "idiotic."

Our schools brand their pupils by a system of marks, while our foremost colleges measure the knowledge and education of their students by the number of "points" passed. The student may pass either in Logic or Blacksmithing. It does not matter which, provided he makes up a certain number of "points"!

College-committees refuse admission to young students of genius, because "it is against the policy and the principles of the university." College-professors expel promising students from the lecture-room for "the good of the class as a whole," because the students "happen to handle their hats in the middle of a lecture." This, you see, interferes with class discipline. *Fiat justitia, pereat mundus.* Let genius perish, provided the system lives. Why not suppress all genius, as a disturbing element, for "the good of the classes," for the weal of the commonwealth? Education of man and cultivation of genius, indeed! This is not school policy.

We school and drill our children and youth in schoolma'am mannerism, schoolmaster mind-ankylosis, school-superintendent stiff-joint ceremonialism, factory regulations and office-discipline. We give our pupils and students artisan-inspiration and business-spirituality. Originality is suppressed. Individuality is crushed. Mediocrity is at a premium. That is why our country has such clever business men, such cunning artisans, such resourceful politicians, such adroit leaders of new cults, but no scientists, no artists, no philosophers, no statesmen, no genuine talent and no true genius.

School-teachers have in all ages been mediocre in intellect and incompetent. Leibnitz is regarded as a dullard and Newton is considered as a blockhead. Never, however, in the history of mankind have school teachers fallen to such a low level of mediocrity as in our times and in our country. For it is not the amount of knowledge that counts in true education, but originality and independence of thought that are of importance in education. But independence and originality of ,thought are just the very elements that are suppressed by our modern barrack-system of education. No wonder that military men claim that the best "education" is given in military schools.

We are not aware that the incubus of officialdom, and the succubus of bureaucracy have taken possession of our schools. The red tape of officialdom, like a poisonous weed, grows luxuriantly in our schools and chokes the life of our young generation. Instead of growing into a people of great independent thinkers, the nation is in danger of fast becoming a crowd of well-drilled, well-disciplined, commonplace individuals, with strong philistine habits and notions of hopeless mediocrity.

In levelling education to mediocrity we imagine that we uphold the democratic spirit of our institutions. Our American sensibilities a-re shocked when the president of one of our leading colleges dares to recommend to his college that it should cease catering to the average student. "We think it un-American, rank treason to our democratic spirit when a college president has the courage to proclaim the principle that "To form the mind and character of one man of marked talent, not to say genius, would be worth more to the community which he would serve than the routine training of hundreds of undergraduates."

We are optimistic, we believe in the pernicious superstition that genius needs no help, that talent will take care of itself. Our kitchen clocks and dollar timepieces need careful handling, but our chronometers and astronomical clocks can run by themselves.

The truth is, however, that the purpose of the school and the college is not to create an intellectual aristocracy, but to educate, to bring out the individuality, the originality, the latent powers of talent and genius present in what we unfortunately regard as "the average student." Follow Mill's advice. Instead of aiming at athletics, social connections, vocations and generally at the professional art of money-making, "Aim at something noble. Make your system such that a great man may be formed by it, and there will be a manhood in your little men, of which you do not dream."

Awaken in early childhood the critical spirit of man; awaken, early in the child's life, love of knowledge, love of truth, of art and literature for their own sake, and you arouse man's genius. We have average mediocre students, because we have mediocre teachers, department-store superintendents, clerkly principals and deans with bookkeepers' souls, because our schools and colleges deliberately aim at mediocrity.

Ribot in describing the degenerated Byzantine Greeks tells us that their leaders were mediocrities and their great men commonplace personalities. Is the American nation drifting in the same direction? It was the system of cultivation of independent thought that awakened the Greek mind to its highest achievements in arts, science and philosophy; it was the deadly Byzantine bureaucratic red tape with its cut-and-dried theological discipline that dried up the sources of Greek genius. We are in danger of building up a Byzantine empire with large institutions and big corporations, small minds and dwarfed individualities. Like the Byzantines we begin to value administration above individuality and official, red-tape ceremonialism above originality.

We wish even to turn our schools into practical school-shops. We shall in time become a nation of well-trained clerks and artisans. The time is at hand when hall be justified in writing over the gates of our school-shops "mediocrity made here!"

CHAPTER NINE

I ASSUME that as liberal men and women you have no use for the process of cramming and stuffing of college-geese and mentally indolent, morally obtuse and religiously "cultured" prigs and philistines, but that you realize that your true vocation is to get access to the latent energies of your children, to stimulate their reserve energies and educate, bring to light, man's genius. The science of psychopathology now sets forth a fundamental principle which is not only of the utmost importance in psychotherapeutics, but also in the domain of education; it is the principle of stored up, dormant, reserve energy, the principle of potential, subconscious, reserve energy.

It is claimed on good evidence, biological, physiological and psychopathological, that man possesses large stores of unused energy which the ordinary stimuli of life are not only unable to reach, but even tend to inhibit. Unusual combinations of circumstances, however, radical changes of the environment, often unloose the inhibitions brought about by the habitual narrow range of man's interests and surroundings. Such unloosening of inhibitions helps to release fresh supplies of reserve energy. It is not the place here to discuss this fundamental principle; I can only state it in the most general way, and give its general trend in the domain of education.

You have heard the psychologizing educator advise the formation of good, fixed, stable habits in early life. Now I want to warn you against the dangers of such unrestricted advice. Fixed adaptations, stable habits, tend to raise the thresholds of mental life, tend to inhibit the liberation, the output of reserve-energy. Avoid routine. Do not let your pupils fall into the ruts of habits and customs. Do not let even the best of habits harden beyond the point of further possible modification.

Where there is a tendency towards formation of over-abundant mental cartilage, set your pupils to work under widely different circumstances. Confront them with a changed set of conditions. Keep them on the move. Surprise them by some apparently paradoxical relations and strange phenomena. Do not let them settle down to one definite set of actions or reactions. Remember that rigidity, like sclerosis, induration of tissue, means decay of originality, destruction of man's genius. With solidified and invariable habits not only does the reserve energy become entirely inaccessible, but the very individuality is extinguished.

Do not make of our children a nation of philistines. Why say, you make man in your own image? Do not make your schools machine-shops, turning out on one uniform pattern so much mediocrity per year. Cultivate variability. The tendency towards variability is the most precious part of a good education. Beware of the philistine with his set, stable habits.

The important principle in education is not so much *formation* of habits as the power of their re-formation. The power of breaking up habits is by far the more essential factor of a good education. It is in this power of breaking down habits that we can find the key for the unlocking of the otherwise inaccessible stores of subconscious reserve energy. *The cultivation of the power of habit-disintegration is what constitutes the proper education of man's genius.*[1]

---

1. A well known editor of one of the academic Journals on Educational Psychology writes to me as follows: "Your remarks on the avoidance of routine would be like a red rag to a bull for a number of educators who are emphasizing the importance of habit formation in education at present."

CHAPTER TEN

THE power of breaking down or dissolving habits depends on the amount and strength of the *aqua fortis* of the intellect. The logical and critical activities of the individual should be cultivated with special care. The critical self, as we may put it, should have control over the automatic and the subconscious. For the subconscious has been shown to form the fertile soil for the breeding of the most dangerous germs of mental disease, epidemics, plagues and pestilences in their worst forms. We should try to develop the individual's critical abilities in early childhood, not permitting the suggestible subconsciousness to predominate, and to become overrun with noxious weeds and pests.

We should be very careful with the child's critical self, as it is weak and has little resistance. We should, therefore, avoid all dominating authority and categorical imperative commands. Autocratic authority cultivates in the child the predisposition to abnormal suggestibility, to hypnotic states, and leads towards the dominance of the subconscious with its train of pernicious tendencies and deleterious results.

There is a period in the child's life between the ages of five and ten when he is very inquisitive, asking all kinds of questions. *It is the age of discussion in the child.* This inquisitiveness and discussion should by all means be encouraged and fostered. We should aid the development of the spirit of inquisitiveness and curiosity in the child. For this is the acquisition of control over the stored-up, latent energies of man's genius.

We should not arrest the child's questioning spirit, as we are often apt to do, but should strongly encourage the apparently meddlesome and troublesome searching and prying and scrutinizing of *whatever interests the child.* Everything should be open to the child's searching interest; nothing should be suppressed and tabooed as too sacred for examination. The spirit of inquiry, the genius of man, is more sacred than any abstract belief, dogma and creed.

A rabbi came to ask my advice about the education of his little boy. My advice was: "Teach him not to be a Jew." The man of God departed and never came again. The rabbi did not care for education, but for faith. He did not wish his boy to become a man, but to be a Jew.

The most central, the most crucial part of the education of man's genius is *the knowledge, the recognition of evil* in all its protean forms and innumerable disguises, intellectual, æsthetic and moral, such as fallacies, sophisms, ugliness, deformity, prejudice, superstition, vice and depravity. Do not be afraid to discuss these matters with the child. For the knowledge, the recognition of evil does not only possess the virtue of immunization of the child's mind against all evil, but furnishes the main power for habit disintegration with consequent release and control of potential reserve energy, of manifestations of human genius. When a man becomes contented and ceases to notice the evils of life, as is done by some modern religious sects, he loses his hold on the powers of man's genius, he loses touch with the throbbing pulse of humanity, he loses hold on reality and falls into subhuman groups.

The purpose of education, of a *liberal* education, is not to live in a fool's paradise, or to go through the world in a post-hypnotic state of negative hallucinations. The true aim of a liberal education is, as the Scriptures put it, to have the *eyes opened,*—to be free from all delusions, illusions, from the *fata morgana* of life. We prize a liberal education, because it *liberates* us from subjection to superstitious fears, delivers us from the narrow bonds of prejudice, from the exalted or depressing delusions of moral paresis, intellectual dementia-praecox, and religious paranoia. A liberal education liberates us from the enslavement to the degrading influence of *all* idol-worship.

In the education of man do not play on his subconscious sense by deluding him by means of hypnotic and post-hypnotic suggestions of positive and negative hallucinations, with misty and mystic, beatific visions. Open his *eyes* to undisguised reality. Teach him, show him how to strip the real from its unessential wrappings and adornments and see things in their nakedness. *Open the eyes of your children so that they shall see, understand and face courageously the evils of life.*

Then will you do your duty as parents, then will you give your children the proper education.

CHAPTER ELEVEN

I HAVE spoken of the fundamental law of early education. The question is *"how early?"* There are, of course, children who are backward in their development. This backwardness may either be congenital or may be due to some overlooked pathological condition that may be easily remedied by proper treatment. In the large majority of children, however, the beginning of education *is between the second and third year.* It is at that time that the child begins to form his interests. It is at that critical period that we have to seize the opportunity to guide the child's formative energies in the right channels. To delay is a mistake and a wrong to the child. We can at that early period awaken a love of knowledge which will persist through life. The child will as eagerly play in the game of knowledge as he now spends the most of his energies in meaningless games and objectless silly sports.

We claim we are afraid to force the child's mind. We claim we are afraid *to strain his brain prematurely.* This is an error. In *directing* the course of the use of the child's energies we do not force the child. If *you* do not *direct* the energies in the right course, the child will *waste* them in the wrong direction. The same amount of mental energy used in those silly games, which we think are specially adapted for the childish mind, can be directed, with lasting benefit, to the development of his *interests in intellectual activity and love of knowledge. The child will learn to play at the game of knowledge-acquisition with the same ease, grace and interest as he is showing now in his nursery-games and physical exercises.*

CHAPTER TWELVE

ARISTOTLE laid it down as a self-evident proposition that all Hellenes *love knowledge*. This was true of the national genius of the ancient Greeks. The love of wisdom is the pride of the ancient Greek in contradistinction to the barbarian, who does not prize knowledge. We still belong to the barbarians. Our children, our pupils, our students have no love of knowledge.

The ancient Greeks knew the value of a good education and understood its fundamental elements. They laid great stress on early education and they knew how to develop man's mental energies, without fear of injury to the brain and physical constitution. The Greeks were not afraid of thought, that it might injure the brain. 'They were strong men, great thinkers.

The love of knowledge, the love of truth for its own sake, is entirely neglected in our modern schemes of education. Instead of training men we train mechanics, artisans and shopkeepers. We turn our national schools, high schools and universities into trade-schools and machine-shops. The school, whether lower or higher, has now one purpose in view, and that is the training of the pupil in the art of money-making. Is it a wonder that the result is a low form of mediocrity, a dwarfed and crippled specimen of humanity?

Open the reports of our school superintendents and you find that the illustrations setting forth the prominent work performed by the school represent carpentry, shoemaking, blacksmithing, bookkeeping, typewriting, dressmaking, millinery and cookery. One wonders whether it is the report of a factory inspector, the "scientific" advertisement of some instrument-maker or machine-shop, a booklet of some popular hotel, or an extensive circular of some large department-store. Is this what our modern education consists in? Is the aim of the nation to form at its expense vast reserve armies of skilled mechanics, great numbers of well-trained cooks and well-behaved clerks? Is the purpose of the nation to form cheap skilled labor for the manufacturer, or is the aim of society to form intelligent, educated citizens?

The high-school and college courses advised by

the professors and elected by the student are with reference to the vocation in life, to business and to trade. Our schools, our high schools, our colleges and universities are all animated with the same sordid aim of giving electives for early specialization in the art of money-getting. We may say with Mill that our schools and colleges give no true education, no true culture. We drift to the status of Egypt and India with their castes of early trained mechanics, professionals and shopkeepers. Truly educated men we shall have none. We shall become a nation of narrow-minded philistines, well contented with their mediocrity. The savage compresses the skull of the infant, while we flatten the brain and cramp the mind of our young generation.

CHAPTER THIRTEEN

THE great thinker, John Stuart Mill, insists that "the great business of every rational being is the strengthening and enlarging of his own intellect and character. The empirical knowledge which the world demands, which is the stock in trade of money-getting, we would leave the world to provide for itself." We must make our system of education such "that a great man may be formed by it, and there will be a manhood in your little men of which you do not dream. We must have a system of education capable of forming great minds." Education must aim at the bringing out of the genius in man. Do we achieve such aim by the formation of philistine-specialists and young petty-minded artisans?

"The very cornerstone of an education," Mill

tells us, "intended to form great minds, must be the recognition of the principle, that the object is to call forth the greatest possible quantity of intellectual power, and to inspire the intensest *love of truth; and this without a particle of regard to the results to which the exercise of that power may lead.*" With us the only love of truth is the one that leads to the shop, the bank and the counting-house.

The home controls the school and the college. As long as the home is dominated by commercial ideals, the school will turn out mediocre tradesmen.

This, however, is one of the characteristic types of the American home: the mother thinks of dresses, fashions and parties. The daughter twangs and thrums on the piano, makes violent attempts at singing that sound as "the crackling of thorns under a pot," is passionately fond of shopping, dressing and visiting. Both mother and daughter, love society, show and gossip. The father works in some business or at some trade and loves sports and games. Not a spark of refinement and culture, not a redeeming ray of love of knowledge and of art, lighting up the commonplace and frivolous life of the family. What wonder that the children of ten and eleven can hardly read and write, are little brutes and waste away their precious life of childhood in the close, dusty, overheated rooms of the early grades of some elementary school? Commercial mediocrity is raised at home and cultivated in the school.

"As a means of educating the many, the universities are absolutely null," exclaims Mill. "The attainments of any kind required for taking all the degrees conferred by these bodies are, at Cambridge, utterly contemptible." Our American schools, with their ideals of money-earning capacities, our colleges glorying in their athletics, football teams and courses for professional and business specializations would have been regarded by Mill as below contempt.

What indeed is the worth of an education that does not create even as much as an ordinary respect for learning and love of truth, and that prizes knowledge in terms of hard cash? What is the educational worth of a college or of a university which suppresses its most gifted students by putting them under the ban of disorderly behavior, because of not conforming to commonplace mannerisms? What is the educational value of a university which is but a modern edition of a gladiatorial school with a smattering of the humanities? What is the educational value of an institution of learning that expels its best students because they "attract more attention than their professors"? What is the intellectual level of a college that expels from its courses the ablest of its students for some slight infringement, and that an involuntary one, under the pretext that it is done for the sake of class-discipline, "for the general good of the class" What travesty on education is a system that suppresses genius in the interest of mediocrity? What is the cultural, the humanistic value of an education that puts a prize on mediocrity?

CHAPTER FOURTEEN

DISCIPLINE, fixed habits approved by the pedagogue are specially enforced in our schools. To this may be added some "culture" in the art of money-getting in the case of the boys, while in the case of girls the æsthetic training of millinery and dressmaking may be included. The colleges, in addition to class-discipline looked after by the professors and college-authorities, are essentially an organization of hasty-pudding clubs, football associations and athletic corporations. What is the use of a college if not for its games? Many regard the college as useful for the formation of business acquaintances in later life. Others again consider the college a good place for learning fine manners. In other words, the college and the school are for athletics, good manners, business companionship, mechanical arts and money-getting. They are for anything but education.

We have become so used to college athletics that it appears strange and possibly absurd to demand of a college the cultivation of man's genius. Who expects to find an intellectual atmosphere among the great body of our college undergraduates? Who expects of our schools and colleges true culture and the cultivation of a taste for literature, art and science? A dean, an unusually able man, of one of the prominent Eastern colleges tells me that he and his friends are very pessimistic about his students and especially about the great body of undergraduate students. Literature, art, science have no interest for the student; games and athletics fill his mental horizon.

In the training of our children, in the education of our young, we think that discipline, obedience to paternal and maternal commands, whether rational or absurd, are of the utmost importance. "We do not realize that in such a scheme of training we fail to cultivate the child's critical faculties, but only succeed in suppressing the child's individuality. We only break his will-power and originality. We also prepare the ground for future nervous and mental maladies characterized by their fears, indecisions, hesitations, diffidence, irritability, lack of individuality and absence of self-control.

We laugh at the Chinese, because they bandage

the feet of their girls, we ridicule those who cripple their chest and mutilate their figure by the tight lacing of their corsets, but we fail to realize the baneful effects of submitting the young minds to the grindstone of our educational discipline. I have known good fathers and mothers who have unfortunately been so imbued with the necessity of disciplining the child that they have crushed the child's spirit in the narrow bonds of routine and custom. How can we expect to get great men and women when from infancy we train our children to conform to the philistine ways of Mrs. Grundy?

In our schools and colleges, habits, discipline and behavior are specially emphasized by our teachers, instructors and professors. Our deans and professors think more of reel tape, of "points," of discipline than of study; they think more of authoritative suggestion than of critical instruction. The pedagogue fashions the pupil after his own image. The professor, with his disciplinarian tactics, forces the student into the imbecile mummy-like mannerism of Egyptian pedantry and into the barrack-regulations of class-etiquette. Well may professors of our "war-schools" claim that the best education is given in military academies: They are right, if discipline is education. But why not the reformatory, the asylum and the prison?

We trust our unfortunate youth to the Procrustean bed of the mentally obtuse, hide-bound pedagogue. We desiccate, sterilize, petrify and embalm our youth in keeping with the rules of our Egyptian code and in accordance with the Confucian regulations of our school-clerks and college mandarins. Our children learn by rote and are guided by routine.

CHAPTER FIFTEEN

BEING in a barbaric stage, we are afraid of thought. We are under the erroneous belief that thinking, study, causes nervousness and mental disorders. In my practice as physician in nervous and mental diseases, I can say without hesitation that I have not met a single case of nervous or mental trouble caused by too much thinking or over study. This is at present the opinion of the best psychopathologists. What produces nervousness is worry, emotional excitement and lack of interest in the work. But that is precisely what we do with our children. We do not take care to develop a love of knowledge in their early life for fear of brain injury, and then when it is late to acquire the interest, we force them to study, and we cram them and feed them and stuff them like geese. What you often get is fatty degeneration of the mental liver.

If, however, you do not neglect the child between the second and third year, and see to it that the brain should not be starved, should have its proper function, like the rest of the bodily organs, by developing an interest in intellectual activity and love of knowledge, no forcing of the child to study is afterwards requisite. The child will go on by himself,—he will derive intense enjoyment from his intellectual activity, as he does from his games and physical exercise. The child will be stronger, healthier, sturdier than the present average child, with its purely animal activities and total neglect of brain function. His physical and mental development will go a pace. He will not be a barbarian with animal proclivities and a strong distaste for knowledge and mental enjoyment, but he will be a strong, healthy, *thinking man*.

Besides, many a mental trouble will be prevented in adult-life. The child will acquire knowledge with the same ease as he learns to ride the bicycle or play ball. By the tenth year, without almost any effort, the child will acquire the knowledge which at present the best college-graduate obtains with infinite labor and pain. That this can be accomplished I can say with authority; I know it as a fact from my own experience with child-life.

From an economical standpoint alone, think of

the saving it would ensure for society. Consider the fact that our children spend nearly eight years in the common school, studying spelling and arithmetic, and do not know them when they graduate! Think of the eight years of waste of school buildings and salaries for the teaching force. However, our real object is not economy, but the development of a strong, healthy, great race of genius.

As fathers and mothers it may interest you to learn of one of those boys who were brought up in the love and enjoyment of knowledge for its own sake. At the age of twelve, when other children of his age are hardly able to read and spell, and drag a miserable mental existence at the apron strings of some antiquated school-dame, the boy is intensely enjoying courses in the highest branches of mathematics and astronomy at one of our foremost universities. The Iliad and the Odyssey are known to him by heart, and he is deeply interested in the advanced work of Classical Philology. He is able to read Herodotus, Æschylus, Sophocles, Euripides, Aristophanes, Lucian and other Greek writers with the same zest and ease as our schoolboy reads his Robinson Crusoe or the productions of Cooper and Henty. The boy has a fair understanding of Comparative Philology and Mythology. He is well versed in Logic, Ancient History, American History and has a general insight into our politics and into the groundwork of our Constitution. At the same time he is of an extremely happy disposition, brimming over with humor and fun. His physical condition is splendid, his cheeks glow. with health. Many a girl would envy his complexion. Being above five feet four he towers above the average boy or his age. His physical constitution, weight, form and hardihood of organs, far surpasses that of the ordinary schoolboy. He looks like a boy of sixteen. He is healthy, strong and sturdy.

The philistine-pseudogogues, the self-contented school-autocrats are so imbued with the fear of intellectual activity and with the superstitious dread of early mental education, they are so obsessed with the morbid phobia of human reflective powers, they are so deluded by the belief that study causes disease that they eagerly adhere to the delusion, to quote from a school-superintendent's letter, about the boy being "in a sanitarium, old and worn-out." No doubt, the cramming, the routine, the rote, the mental and moral tyranny of the principal and school-superintendent do tend to nervous degeneracy and mental break-down. Poor old college owls, academic barn-yard-fowls and worn-out sickly school-bats, you are panic-stricken by the power of sunlight, you are in agonizing, in mortal terror of critical, reflective thought, you dread and suppress the genius of the young.

We do not appreciate the genius harbored in the average child, and we let it lie fallow. We are mentally poor, not because we lack riches, but because we do not know how to use the wealth of mines, the hidden treasures, the now inaccessible mental powers which we possess.

In speaking of our mental capacities, Francis Galton, I think, says that we are in relation to the ancient Greeks what the Bushmen and Hottentots are in relation to us. Galton and many other learned men regard the modern European races as inferior to the Hellenic race. They are wrong, and I know from experience that they are wrong. It rests in our hands either to remain inferior barbarians or to rival and even surpass in brilliancy the genius of the ancient Hellenes. We can develop into a great race by the proper education of man's genius.

CHAPTER SIXTEEN

ONE other important point claims our attention in the process of education of man's genius. We must immunize our children against mental microbes, as we vaccinate our babies against small-pox. *The cultivation of critical judgment and the knowledge of evil are two powerful constituents that form the antitoxin for the neutralization of the virulent toxins produced by mental microbes.* At the same time we should not neglect proper conditions of mental hygiene. "We should not people the child's mind with ghost-stories, with absurd beliefs in the supernatural, and with articles of creed charged with brimstone and pitch from the bowels of hell. *We must guard the child against all evil fears, superstitions, prejudices and credulity.*

We should counteract the baneful influences of

the pathogenic, pestiferous, mental microbes which now infest our social air, since the child, not having yet formed the antitoxin of critical judgment and knowledge of evil, has not the power of resisting mental infection, and is thus very susceptible to mental contagion on account of his extreme suggestibility. The cultivation of credulity, the absence of critical judgment and of recognition of evil, with consequent increase of suggestibility, make man an easy prey to all kinds of social delusions, mental epidemics, religious crazes, financial manias, and political plagues, which have been the baleful pest of aggregate humanity in all ages.

The immunization of children, the development of resistance to mental germs whether moral, immoral or religious, can only be effected by the medical man with a psychological and psychopathological training. Just as science, philosophy and art have gradually passed out of the control of the priest, so now we find that the control of mental and moral life is gradually passing away from under the influence of the church into the hands of the medical psychopathologist.

As we look forward into the future we begin to see that the school is coming under the control of the medical man. The medical man free from superstitions and prejudices, possessed of the science of mind and body, is to assume in the future the supervision of the education of the nation.

The schoolmaster and the schoolma'am with their narrow-minded, pedantic pseudogogics are gradually losing prestige and passing away, while the medical man alone is able to cope with the serious threatening danger of national mental degeneration. Just as the medical profession now saves the nation from physical degeneration and works for the' physical regeneration of the body-politic, so will the medical profession of the future assume the duty of saving the nation from mental and moral decline, from degeneration into a people of fear-possessed, mind-racked psychopathies and neurotics, with broken wills and crushed individualities on the one hand, accompanied, on the other hand, by the still worse affliction and incurable malady of a self-contented mediocrity and a hopeless, Chinese philistinism.

There are in the United States about two hundred thousand insane, while the victims of psychopathic, mental maladies may be counted by the millions. Insanity can be greatly alleviated, but much, if not all, of that psychopathic mental misery known as functional mental disease is entirely preventable. It is the result of our pitiful, wretched, brain-starving, mind-crippling methods of education.

CHAPTER SEVENTEEN

IN my work of mental and nervous diseases I become more and more convinced of the preponderant influence of early childhood in the causation of psychopathic mental maladies. *Most, in fact all, of those functional mental diseases originate in early childhood.* A couple of concrete cases will perhaps best illustrate my point:

The patient is a young man of 26. He suffers from intense melancholic depression, often amounting to agony. He is possessed by the fear of having committed the unpardonable sin. He thinks that he is damned to suffer tortures in hell for all eternity. I cannot go here into the details of the case, but an examination of dread of the unknown, from claustrophobia, fear of remaining alone, fear of darkness and numerous other fears and insistent ideas, into the details of which I cannot go here. By means of the hypnoidal state the symptoms were traced to impressions of early childhood; when at the age of five, the patient was suddenly confronted by a maniacal woman. The child was greatly frightened, and since that time she became possessed by the fear of insanity. When the patient gave birth to her child, she was afraid the child would become insane; many a time she even had a feeling that the child was insane. Thus the fear of insanity is traced to an experience of early childhood, an experience which, having become subconscious, is manifesting itself persistently in the patient's consciousness:

The patient's parents were very religious, and the child was brought up not only in the fear of God, but also in the fear of hell and the devil. Being sensitive and imaginative, the devils of the gospel were to her stern realities. She had a firm belief in "diabolical possessions" and "unclean spirits"; the legend of Jesus exorcising in the country of the Gadarenes unclean spirits, whose name is Legion, was to her a tangible reality. She was brought up on brimstone and pitch, with everlasting fires of the "bottomless pit" for sinners and unbelievers. In the hypnoidal state she clearly remembered the preacher, who used every Sunday to give her the horrors by his picturesque descriptions of the tortures of the "bottomless pit." She was in anguish over the unsolved question: "Do little sinner-girls go to hell?" This fear of hell made the little girl feel depressed and miserable and poisoned many a cheerful moment of her life.

What a lasting effect and what a melancholy gloom this fear of ghosts and of unclean spirits of the bottomless pit produced on this young life may be judged from the following facts: When the patient was about eleven years old, a young girl, a friend of hers, having noticed the patient's fear of ghosts, played on her one of those silly, practical jokes, the effect of which on sensitive natures is often disastrous and lasting. The girl disguised herself as a ghost, in a white sheet, and appeared to the patient, who was just on the point of falling asleep. The child shrieked in terror and fainted. Since that time the patient suffered from nightmares and was mortally afraid to sleep alone; she passed many a night in a state of excitement, frenzied with the fear of apparitions and ghosts.

When about the age of seventeen, she apparently freed herself from the belief in ghosts and unclean powers. But the fear acquired in her childhood did not lapse; it persisted subconsciously and manifested itself in the form of uncontrollable fears. She was afraid to remain alone in a room, especially in the evening. Thus, once when she had to go upstairs alone to pack her trunks, a gauzy garment called forth the experience of her ghost-fright; she had the illusion of seeing a ghost, and fell fainting to the floor. Unless specially treated, fears acquired in childhood last through life.

"Every ugly thing," says Mosso, the great Italian physiologist, "told to the child, every shock, every fright given him, will remain like minute splinters in the flesh, to torture him all his life long.

An old soldier whom I asked what greatest fears had been, answered thus: 'I have only had one, but it pursues me still. I am nearly seventy years old, I have looked death in the face I not know how many times; I have never lost heart in any danger, but when I pass a little old church in the shades of forest, or a deserted chapel in the mountains, I always remember a neglected oratory in my native village, and I shiver and look around, as though seeking the corpse of a murdered man which I once saw carried into it when a child, and with which an old servant wanted to shut me up to make me good.' Here, too, experiences of early childhood have persisted subconsciously throughout lifetime.

CHAPTER EIGHTEEN

I APPEAL to you, fathers and mothers, and to you, liberal-minded readers, asking you to turn your attention to the education of your children, to the training of the young generation of future citizens. I do not appeal to our official educators, to our scientific, psychological pseudogogues, to the clerks of our teaching shops,—for they are beyond all hope. From that quarter I expect nothing but attacks and abuse. We cannot possibly expect of the philistine-educator and mandarin pseudogogue the adoption of different views of education. We should not keep new wine in old goat-skins. The present school-system squanders the resources of the country and wastes the energies, the lives of our children. Like Cato our cry should be *Carthago delenda est,*—the school-system should be abolished and with it should go the present psychologizing educator, the schoolmaster and the schoolma'am.

Fathers and mothers, you keep in your hands the fate of the young generation. You are conscious of the great responsibility, of the vast, important task laid upon you by the education of your children. For, according to the character of the training and education given to the young, they may be made a sickly host of nervous wrecks and miserable wretches; or they may be formed into a narrow-minded, bigoted, mediocre crowd of self-contented "cultured" philistines, bat-blind to evil; or they may be made a *great race of genius* with powers of rational control of their latent, potential, reserve energy. The choice remains with you.

APPENDIX: PRECOCITY IN CHILDREN

Reproduced in part, with the kind permission of the publishers, from my contribution to the forthcoming *Encyclopædia and Dictionary of Education*, published by Sir Isaac Pitman and Sons, London, England.

By precocity I mean the manifestation of the child's mental functions at a period earlier than the one observed in the past and present generations of children.

In the course of his growth and development the individual unfolds his inner powers through acquisition of the stored-up experiences of previous generations.

The well known biogenetic law may, with some modifications, be applied to mental life. The devel-

opment of the individual is an abbreviated repro-
duction of the evolution of the species. Briefly put:
Ontogenesis is an epitome of Phylogenesis. This
biogenetic law holds true in the domain of education. The stored-up experiences of the race are con-
densed, foreshortened, and recapitulated in the
child's life history. This process of progressive "precocity," or of foreshortening of education, has been
going on unconsciously in the course of human
evolution. We have reached a stage when man can
be made conscious of this fundamental process,
thus getting control over his own growth and development.

Although the process of foreshortening of education has been taking place throughout the history
of mankind, and especially of civilized humanity,
still the process has remained imperceptible on account of its extremely slow rate of progress. Hence
the fact of "precocity," or of early development of
children, has been hitherto regarded as rare, as phe-
nomenal. Like all rare phenomena, precocity, or
early child development, is considered as unique, as
abnormal, and even as pathological. In fact, many
still regard precocity as some form of malady akin
to mental alienation.

It is well to bear in mind that phenomena, at
first scarce and rare, may under favorable conditions become sufficiently numerous to be quite
common. In fact, we may lay it down as a law that

all discoveries, inventions, and changes in general, economical, political, social, mental, moral, and religious, first appear on a small scale in limited areas from which they spread in various directions. Organisms start, as variations or mutations, from minute nuclei of growth; species have their origin in small centres and restricted areas. A new species may begin with some apparently insignificant variation which may grow and develop, and which, from a certain standpoint, may be regarded as an abnormality.

What at present is considered as "precocity," and hence as an abnormality, may really be the foreshadowing of the future. The apparently precocious variation may and will turn out a normal phenomenon. The stone which the builders refused is become the head stone of the corner. Early education, precocity, is to become the corner stone of human life. At present the preliminary period of child education is unduly retarded to the detriment of the individual and society.

The truth is, we do not realize the importance of early training. We begin education late in the child's life, when dispositions have become formed and habits have become rigid. This delay seriously injures the growth of the child by lowering the level of mental activity. The critical points of formation of mental interests are allowed to slip by, leaving the individual irresponsive to mental, æsthetic, and moral interests. The critical turning points, when the best energies could be brought out, are not taken care of at the right moment.

The mental functions become prematurely atrophied and degenerated. When we later on attempt to awaken those functions, we are surprised to find them absent. We labor under the false impression that the child is naturally inapt and deficient. To make up for this apparent deficiency we force the child's mind into narrow channels, crippling and deforming it into mean mediocrity. The child is run into the rigid moulds of home, school, and college with the result of permanent mutilation of originality and genius. The individual is deformed, because the critical spirit of inquiry and originality is racked on the Procrustes' bed of home and school. The unfortunate thing about it is the firm belief that the crippled spirit of the child is a congenital mediocrity. Instead of shouldering the fault, we put the burden on heredity. Darwinism with its spontaneous variation and hereditary transmission, Austro-Germanic Mendelism, accompanied by a widespread propaganda of Eugenics, have blotted out from view the far more fundamental factors of environment and education which play such a paramount role in man's life.

We may profit by recent studies in Psychopathology. In my investigations I have shown the important role which early child experience plays in the patient's life. Psychopathic affections can be traced to child fears which become afterwards reinforced by unfavorable conditions of life. This is formulated in my works on psychopathology. Psychopathology clearly brings out the significant fact that a good start in early childhood is of the utmost consequence to the individual. Only a good education in early life can save man from the innumerable psychopathic maladies to which he is subject. The seeds of vicious habits and of criminal tendencies can be eliminated in early childhood.

Early development or what is termed "precocity" in children will not only prevent vice, crime, and disease, but will strengthen the individual along all lines, physical, mental, and moral. We should be careful not to cast the child's mind into ready made moulds, not to subject his mind, his character to the yoke of meaningless mannerisms and rigid formalities. We should have respect for the child's personality. We should remember that there is genius in every healthy, normal child.

We are blind to the child's latent genius, because we look to brute force as our standard. Like savages, we are afraid of genius, especially when it is manifested as "precocity in children." This abject fear of genius and of precocity is one of the most pernicious philistine superstitions, causing the retardation of the progress of humanity. The fear of mental precocity is essentially the phobia of the inveterate philistine.

We should bear in mind that the philistine is an insignificant, though exact part of a huge social machine, of a Frankenstein "kultur" before which the philistine prostrates himself in dust, a social monster of which he is proud to form an irresponsible mite. Whether he be an atom of a political organization, of a nation, or of a military kultur-system, the philistine is trained to be content to play the same ignoble, slavish role of submission, obedience, and irresponsibility. Without personal conscience, without personal will, without personal initiative, the impersonal philistine is like the stupid genie of Aladdin's lamp who slavishly obeys the master of the magic lamp.

The present horrible European war (predicted in this volume several years before the onset of the war. See pp. 30, 31) is the unfortunate, but natural outcome of philistine education and philistine life. The immediate cause of the war may be traced to politics, greed, competition, to commercial, industrial, cultural, national, international, and racial complications. At bottom, however, the present European war is ultimately due to our pernicious system of training, the bane of our industrial, social life. Millions of men are drilled and disciplined to act as automata; men are trained from childhood, at home, school, college, and university to surrender their individual judgment, and follow blindly an alleged "social consciousness," entrusted, by a set of philistine bureaucrats, to superior leaders, to generals, admirals, and field-marshals. Men are hypnotized by a pernicious and vicious system of training and quasi-education to consider it a high, sacred ideal to obey implicitly the will of a few officials and diplomats, to attack, plunder and slaughter at the command of generals and officers, in the interest of a plutocratic oligarchy, hallowed by the vague shibboleth: "Flag, Country, Patriotism."[1] The youth of nations is debauched with the belief in the supreme grandeur of delivering their personal responsibility in the keeping of a handful of Byzantine bureaucrats, irresponsible junkers, and half-crazed Cæsars.

The principle "Be Childlike" is paramount in the education of mankind. The child represents the future, all the possibilities, all the coming greatness of the human race. We, the adults, are contaminated by the brutal passions and vices incident to the struggle for existence and self-preservation.

Plasticity of mind is characteristic of genius. Plasticity of mind and body is preeminently characteristic of the child. Adaptability and plasticity are found in all young tissue, muscle, gland, and nerve. As the organism ages, becomes differentiated, and adapted to special functions and conditions of life, it loses its original plasticity. The tissues become fixed and the functions set. The adult's brain and mind begin to work in ruts. The child is superior to the adult.

The child looks at the world with eyes simple, clear, bright, not blinded by the heavy scales of traditions, superstitions, and prejudices of remote ages. The intricate worries, complex fears, selfish motives, brutal passions, greed, revenge, malice, vice, enmity do not as yet mar the soul of the child. Artificial needs, strong animal passions have no firm hold on the child's mind. The child's mind is purer, fresher, brighter, far more original than the adult intelligence with its philistine notions and hide-bound habits of thought and belief.

With age the mind becomes specialized and degraded in quality. Unless checked by a good education and by a persistent course of mental activity, intellectual and other mental interests, the adult mind is apt to deteriorate. Unless controlled by a good education and by intense mental interests, free from service to animal needs, the emotions of self-regard, the impulse of self-preservation with its fear instinct gradually gain in man the upper hand. In the child, on the contrary, the personal interests are relatively weak, and fluctuating, hence the possibility of pure disinterestedness, pure curiosity, love of learning, the root of all originality present both in genius and the child. The child presents the innocence and gentleness of human genius, the adult philistine is the embodiment of the force and cunning of the brute.

We should not be scared by the bug-bear of precocity. We should awaken man's genius by giving the child an early, a "precocious" education. We should bear in mind that the knowledge of our schoolboys and schoolgirls far surpasses that of the ancient sages or of the mediæval doctors. We should learn to understand and to utilize the process of progressive foreshortening of race acquisitions in the history of the individual.

The great biologist, Professor C. S. Minot, comes to a similar conclusion, as the result of his profound biological investigations: "I believe," says Minot, "that this principle of psychological development, paralleling the career of physical development, needs to be more considered in arranging our educational plans. For if it be true that the decline in the power of learning is most rapid at first, it is evident that we want to make as much use of the early years as possible—that the tendency, for instance, which has existed in many of our universities, to postpone the period of entrance into college, is biologically an erroneous tendency. It would be better to have the young man get to college earlier, graduate earlier, get into practical life or into professional schools earlier, while the power of learning is greater."

I may say that within my experience children

who had the advantage of an early education and training manifested a higher grade of intellectual and moral life, a far better state of physical health than children brought up under the present retarding and crippling system of education. In conclusion I may add that in order to gain access to man's Reserve Energy we must have recourse to early child education, to the much maligned, and greatly feared "Precocity in Children."

---

1. "The cheapest' form of pride," says Schopenhauer, "is national pride; for if a man is proud of his own nation it follows that he has no qualities of his own of which he can be proud; otherwise, he would not have recourse to those which he shares with his fellow-men. . . . Every miserable fool who has nothing at all of which he can be proud adopts as a last resource pride in the nation to which he belongs; he is ready and glad to defend all its faults and follies, tooth and nail, thus reimbursing himself for his inferiority. . . .National character is only another name for the particular form which the littleness, perversity, and baseness of mankind take in every country.". . . "Narrowness, prejudice, vanity, and self-interest are the main elements of patriotism." . . . "Does not all history show that whenever a king is firmly established on the throne, and the people reach some degree of prosperity, he uses it to lead an army, like a band of robbers, against adjoining countries? Are not almost all wars ultimately undertaken for purpose of plunder?" . . . Schopenhauer prophetically warns his countrymen: "All war is a matter of robbery, and the Germans should take that as a warning."